CLIFTON PARK

W9-AYQ-952

BIKE SAFETY

by Emma Bassier

Cody Koala
An Imprint of Pop!
popbooksonline.com

abdobooks.com

Published by Pop!, a division of ABDO, PO Box 398166, Minneapolis, Minnesota 55439.
Printed in the United States of America, North Mankato, Minnesota

052020
092020

THIS BOOK CONTAINS RECYCLED MATERIALS

Cover Photo: iStockphoto
Interior Photos: iStockphoto, 1, 5, 7 (bottom left), 15, 17 (top), 17 (bottom right), 18; Shutterstock Images, 7 (top), 7 (bottom right), 8, 11, 13, 17 (bottom left), 21

Editor: Connor Stratton
Series Designer: Christine Ha

Library of Congress Control Number: 2019954990

Publisher's Cataloging-in-Publication Data

Names: Bassier, Emma, author.
Title: Bike safety / by Emma Bassier
Description: Minneapolis, Minnesota : POP!, 2021 | Series: Safety for kids | Includes online resources and index.
Identifiers: ISBN 9781532167515 (lib. bdg.) | ISBN 9781532168611 (ebook)
Subjects: LCSH: Cycling--Safety measures--Juvenile literature. | Bicycles and tricycles--Juvenile literature. | Traffic safety--Juvenile literature. | Safety education--Juvenile literature. | Accidents--Prevention--Juvenile literature.
Classification: DDC 796.6/028--dc23

Hello! My name is

Cody Koala

Pop open this book and you'll find QR codes like this one, loaded with information, so you can learn even more!

Scan this code* and others like it while you read, or visit the website below to make this book pop.

popbooksonline.com/bike-safety

*Scanning QR codes requires a web-enabled smart device with a QR code reader app and a camera.

Table of Contents

Riding a Bike

Padma stops her bike at a street corner. She looks both ways. Padma makes sure no cars are coming. Then she crosses the street. She is biking safely.

Watch a video here!

5

Ready to Ride

Before riding, have an adult help check the bike. Test the brakes. Make sure the chain isn't broken. And make sure the tires aren't flat.

Some bikes brake by pedaling backwards. Others have brake levers on the handlebars.

brake lever

Learn more here!

Always wear a helmet.
A helmet protects your head
if you fall. Make sure your
helmet fits. It should cover
your forehead. The chin
strap should not be too tight.
You can also wear pads on
your elbows and knees.

Don't ride barefoot. Wear sneakers. Dress in bright-colored clothes. Use **reflective** stripes on your clothing, bike, or backpack. These stripes will help drivers see you.

Chapter 3

Rules of the Road

Plan a **route** before leaving. Choose bike paths and roads with less traffic. **Obey** traffic lights and signs. Ride in the same direction as cars.

Complete an
activity here!

Keep your hands on the handlebars at all times. Only take them off to use hand **signals**. These signals show when and which way you are turning.

Biking Hand Signals

▶ **Left Turn**

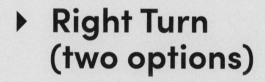

▶ **Right Turn (two options)**

▶ **Stop**

Chapter 4

Being Careful

Stay **alert** while riding. Keep your eyes up and look both ways before crossing a street. Watch for cars pulling in and out of driveways.

Learn more here!

Falls can be dangerous. To stay safe, look where you're going. Watch for holes in the road. Be extra careful on **gravel** or other rough ground.

Ride single file with friends, not side by side. Walk your bike across busy streets. And don't ride your bike at night.

Wearing headphones while riding can make it harder to hear cars.

Making Connections

Text-to-Self

Have you ridden a bike before? If yes, how did you stay safe? If not, how would you stay safe?

Text-to-Text

Have you read other books about safety tips? How were those tips similar to or different from the tips described in this book?

Text-to-World

Riding a bike is one way to travel. People can also take cars, ride buses, or walk. How can they stay safe while traveling in these ways?

Glossary

alert – being watchful and careful.

gravel – a type of ground made from loose bits of rock.

obey – to follow rules or do what a person says.

reflective – able to make light bounce off a surface.

route – a planned way to get from one place to another.

signal – an action that tells other people what will happen next.

Index

Online Resources

popbooksonline.com

Thanks for reading this Cody Koala book!

Scan this code* and others like it in this book, or visit the website below to make this book pop!

popbooksonline.com/bike-safety

*Scanning QR codes requires a web-enabled smart device with a QR code reader app and a camera.